Moonlight Ride

Alexis Beale

MOONLIGHT RIDE

Paperback ISBN: 979-8-218-05772-5

To my mom and Gram,
thank you for always believing in me.

To those that need some healing,
this one's for you.

Let *Moonlight Ride* take you on a cosmic journey through heartbreak, nostalgia, and healing. What you'll find here is a collection of poems, photographs, and songs that capture the most vulnerable moments we all feel while trying to move on.

The poems in this collection follow the process of healing from heartbreak. For me, that process unfolded into three phases, each one corresponding to a chapter of this book: Dusk, Midnight, and Dawn. Dusk represents the initial dark feelings that arise after heartbreak (denial, anger, and sorrow). Midnight highlights the difficulty in coming to terms with the finality of a lost love (nostalgia, over-romanticization, and finally acceptance). Dawn follows the journey of moving on and healing by finding love within yourself, nature, and the universe.

The photographs here were taken in the summer of 2021 during a road trip up the California coast. This trip heavily influenced the final chapter of this book. Over the course of two weeks, I traveled with my closest friends to Malibu, Joshua Tree, Yosemite, Lake Tahoe, and Big Sur. Healing took a new meaning when I found myself immersed in nature and surrounded by the people I love and that love me. These photos were taken on Fujicolor 400 film on my Canon Sure Shot 80u.

I have decided to add a musical component to this book because music has a heavy impact on my art. I wrote most of this book listening to specific albums and collections of songs; if I was able to heal, it is also thanks to that. Through the three playlists I included (one for each section), I wish for you to connect with the poetry – and with that *you,* that *me,* that *us,* who went through the motions of heartbreak can come back even stronger, ascending to a higher state of being.

Tune in to the magic. Feel connected. Let this book take you on a moonlight ride.

All My Love,
Alexis

Each symbol represents the start of a new poem in its respective chapter.

Dusk   Midnight   Dawn

CONTENTS

Moonlight Ride

DUSK

PLAYLIST #1: Dusk

1.   Too Fast – Brent Faiyaz

2.   Ultraviolence – Lana Del Rey

3.   Sad Girl – Lana Del Rey

4.   Crystalised – The XX

5.   Say Something Loving – The XX

6.   Fiction – The XX

7.   High For This – The Weeknd

8.   Wicked Games – The Weeknd

9.   Kiss Land – The Weeknd

10. R U Mine? – Arctic Monkeys

11. Why'd You Only Call Me When You're High?
     – Arctic Monkeys

12. My Propeller – Arctic Monkeys

13. Standing Next To Me – The Last Shadow
     Puppets

14. Calm Like You – The Last Shadow Puppets

See Me

I hope this haunts you.
Take a look at what you did,
you've cast holes all along
the moon's core. They run
deep enough for you to see
what's on the other side. Get closer,
now tell me, what do you see?

Keep looking through me.
All bones and meat. Move whatever
parts you like, don't let me stand
in your way. Keep going,
what do you see?
Are you able to see me?

I should have asked
for those poems back
and all the books
I gave you
that I know
you never read.

Our story is an utter cliché.
I'd like to set fire to it
and watch it burn black.

You can't say you didn't enjoy it,
watching me self-destruct
for the very idea of you.

Waves

I died a romantic.
Dark days in those summer nights
with the pink sand itching at my feet.

I dived in the water, headfirst,
expecting you'd help me float.

Instead, your grip wrapped around
my ankles. I didn't fight you off, or rather
you wouldn't let me go. We both

went under and never
really recovered.

My heart is full.
Something I like is hurting me.

I can feel your warm summer hands
even as the night falls.

We've been together
probably hundreds of times.

Not once did we ever make love.

The streetlamps have blown a fuse
and I've got nothing to lose.

I want you hard, honey. You know
there's no getting over you.

I take you back, each and every time.
I hand you my heart bloodied and raw,

half expecting you to make it all okay.
I know that's not how it works,

but can't we at least try?

You said you loved it
when I read you Sylvia Plath
poems aloud.

You loved it
when I drew circles on your lower back
as you fell asleep.

You loved it
when I played you "Teddy Picker"
by the Arctic Monkeys for the first time.

You loved it
when I wrote you poems on my typewriter
and hid them in the pages of books I let you borrow.

You loved all of it.
        Just not me.

I promise, my love can keep us together
if you'll let it.

       We could be real,
       even if we pretend.

              That could be
         enough
            for
        me.

Toxic Honey

You said you wanted me raw
– emotions and all.

I can't give you that baby,
you should know me better than that by now.

I can't do that, not anymore. Close your eyes
and we can pretend

that I'm her
and you're him.

You love the idea of me,
but not much more. And that's okay,

this isn't something
anyone prays for.

Glass Table Girls

The green ladies tiptoe
into the operating room

to make me
their Hollywood girl.

My mind recoils
at the thought

of them ruining me.
By routine,

they whip out their Stryker saws
to gain exposure to the dura.

Assaulted in their hands,
my wrinkled pink brain folds into silence.

Once they pry it from my skull,
they prick and poke

until every connection I have left
is severed. Stark naked,

they circle my unfavorable limbs
and *tsk* at the oddness:

too flabby, too hairy,
too different.

They collect their reward
and once they fix me up,

the ladies retire,
blood dripping from their boots.

Now,
I am perfect.

Technological Advancements

You are my portal,
my time traveling machine.
With the press of a button, I pretend
to be any person available.
The world around me fades
as I stare, unmoving
until my eyeballs begin to bleed.
I feel my flesh going dry, bones stiffening,
and mind decaying. But I hear
paralysis is correlated to fun
these days.

Strange Fruit

Unsure how to approach it,
he cups it in both hands
and bangs it on the kitchen counter.
He swears it's impenetrable,
what with that thick orange coat
protecting the sacred orb.
But ah, once he finds a crack
he is able to slowly peel back the skin.

She is cold as icebergs
after being locked away
in that white rectangle
almost all her life.
But once naked and exposed,
he sinks his teeth in
and swallows her whole.

You like to bend my brain,
take my words and twist them
on your tongue
until I lose all rational thought.

It's hard to trust myself
       anymore.

They told me it wasn't okay
that you spoke to me that way.

I felt confused —
this was nothing new.

I suppose that was the problem.

You like the feel of
rose water and ivy
wax. Hot and bubbled,
you'd let it drip down
the ends of your finger
and trace shapes
along the curves of my waist.
You like to watch it
paralyze under your thumb.

Shivers glide
       down my spine.

I've learned to memorize
       the echo

from each of your moods
       across the kitchen floor.

This stillness
unsettles me.

Your anger is explosive,
yet I have learned to be the one
to apologize
when your moods resemble Mars.

I let your words take hold
        like cobwebs in my mind.

Their designs
        tracing over mine,

creating connections
        and trapping ugly flies.

You watched them rest there
        and decay what little

I had left
        of myself.

Maybe this has been you from the start
and I'm just now paying attention.

You taught me that obedience
is what love is supposed to feel like.

This isn't a love I care to want.

I've built walls around myself
to keep you out.

Somedays I want you
to hold me in your arms.
That's all.

I feel much lonelier
with you than I do
without.

You bounce back
no matter how far
I push you.

We're a constant ricochet
of I want you –
no, I don't.

This game is maddening
all the same, but

I'll admit,
it keeps me feeling
alive.

I can't see past
these strange horizons.

Which is worse?

Being a second choice
or never being chosen at all?

MIDNIGHT

PLAYLIST #2: Midnight

1. Money Power Glory – Lana Del Rey

2. Islands – The XX

3. I Dare You – The XX

4. Aviation – The Last Shadow Puppets

5. Mykonos – Fleet Foxes

6. Reptilia – The Strokes

7. Lover, Leaver (Taker, Believer) – Greta Van Fleet

8. Edge of Darkness – Greta Van Fleet

9. Age of Machine – Greta Van Fleet

10. I Want You (She's So Heavy) – The Beatles

11. FOR YOUR LOVE – Måneskin

12. Fences – Destroy Boys

13. Charmer And The Snake – The Velveteers

14. Debaser – Pixies

15. Come Here – Dominic Fike

16. Go Your Own Way – Fleetwood Mac

Hypnotic
were your words
as they trickled down my back.

My lips wrap around
the sleek straw of my drink
and I bite down
as images of you flicker
through my mind:

Eyes that melt my insides.
A laugh I treasure.
Cologne that never leaves me.
A body I've kissed.

The wind whispers you love me too.

You

licked

love

notes

down

my

body

without hesitation.

I draw circles along your back,
down your arms,
trying to trace a time
when we were 16:

Young and had yet to break
each other's hearts.

Don't give up on us / not like this / not when you're scared.

Whiskey sours
Moon stars
Neon art
Red lingerie
Your eyes

That's what I want to remember.

Go Slow

before I'm paralyzed.
If you move too quickly
in my direction, I'll only push you
away again. The one
before you taught me that
sudden movements
make it all crumble,
despite good intentions.

Sometimes I bleed words.
Other times I become so reserved,
afraid of seeming too foolish.

Your silence always said more than you ever did.

I fall in love
with people I know
will destroy me
because then,
at least
I see it
coming.

These days I'm not too attached.

Somehow, I must have known
that you would try to use me
and that I would let you every time.

We do this to one another,
knowing full well
what it'll bring.

Do you think we'll get another chance at this?

I don't write happy poems about you.

Vacancy screams
underneath your eyeballs.

My dear, I think my head is floating away.

After a year in isolation,
nothing feels real anymore.

Sit in the silence and let her stir / I've got no feeling.

I never know
which version of you
I am getting.

Why don't you love me
the way (that) I want to be loved?

I clung onto you
because I knew once I let go,
how easily you would
slip away.

You never stuck around for love.

I let myself continue
writing about you.
It's the only way
that I get to keep
a part of you
without hurting
myself.

Sometimes I miss the feeling
of being in love.

Other times, I'm comfortable
with the solitude.

For the most part,
it's painless.

Is this the price I have to pay?
Writing to forget you,
but having our story immortalized
permanently on these pages?

Why is it,
we have these interactions
and I love you all over again
as if nothing happened?
Get out of my head please,
I don't want to love you anymore.
I got rid of you after summer,
but there's something there
in the memories I've buried
[or tried to].
They like to resurface every now and again
and I drown in our old times.
It burns,
the flame we never blew out.
It burns me to my knees.

Nostalgia

Even now, I insist
you're my favorite
almost made it.

I keep waiting
for your memory to fade.
My mind won't let it go.

You were the one thing
I could never
control.

Please tell me how,
what if I can't do this
on my own?

Lunacy strikes,
but I'll swear it's fate
after where we've been.

For you, I'll always surrender.

Happiness fades
and memories deceive.

Sometimes I can't put all the pieces
together.

What we had between us,
was it fate?

Or just a lovely
little daydream?

(I)

I suppose I thought
in the end we'd always come back
to each other, that the timing would be right,
and the stars would circle around us,
fate demanding it was now our time.

(II)

But the sky is dark and those stars in the sky can't possibly be ours because they're dead from millions of years ago. Those aren't our stars, and the timing couldn't ever be right with us because "we" aren't what's right for us. You make me anxious – not in the *I'm so in love and giddy with butterflies sort of way.* You make me anxious to the point where I skip meals waiting for your text, wondering what I did wrong to make you distant. I cry and feel like I'll never recover. You make me feel small and mad at the same time. You play games and tricks to confuse me enough to stay. You leave me heartbroken, yet still in love with you. We're toxic and chaos. Over and over, I go back to you. For some reason I can't detach myself from the idea of what I think we could be, or rather what I think we should be. I want it so badly. I want to not want it. I want to believe that one day I'll stop loving you and not even really think of you. It's been five years now, on and off, and I'm afraid that despite everything, I'll stay.

I'm not entirely sure
that I want to move on.

That would require realizing
it was possible all along

and that we were never
soulmates.

My heart
       still checks up
on you.

Keep my mind sober.
Drag me back to reality if you have to
and let it wash over me,
so that I can breathe again.

No, you won't admit it,
but I've been getting bad again.
Yes, a little mad again.

You made love hurt.

Everyday,
I learn to live
without you.

You were everything when you wanted to be.

What a shame it was so rare and infrequent.

Don't say I love too fast
when it's you who couldn't keep up.

I feel sorry
for this person you've become.

Every time I begin to write,
my pen reaches for your name
as if there were anything more to say.

I don't know how much longer
I can go on writing about a love
that will never be mine.

I wonder if the things I write about you
are even about you anymore.

Sometimes I feel like I am failing myself.

Shouldn't I
be happier?

Shouldn't I
be dating more?

Shouldn't I
be socializing more?

Shouldn't I
be writing more?

Shouldn't I
be more?

Maybe this is sad,

       but sometimes

I have to
remind myself
that I am
loved.

Sex and loneliness kept us together
longer than they should have.

I couldn't love you
and myself.

I had to choose.

Evenings in Venice
where the sun bleeds red
into the ocean
and the air holds me tight.
I'm always mourning
who I used to be.

You were enamored with
a bad nostalgia,

desiring a time that existed
only in our solitude.

Have you found it?
Or is this something you still miss?

I can't love you
like I loved you then.

Ephemeral zip codes
in the cities I have loved
trying to forget you.

We still share the same moon
and even in the stars.
We've been here before.

I might always be yours,
even when I'm out of reach.
I'm yours.

DAWN

PLAYLIST #3: Dawn

1. L.A. – Brent Faiyaz

2. Jealous - Eyedress

3. disco tits – Tove Lo

4. Heater – Flume

5. New Person, Same Old Mistakes – Tame Impala

6. Your Soul – Hippie Sabotage

7. The Way Things Change – Yellow Days

8. French Press – Rolling Blackouts Coastal Fever

9. Eternal Summer – The Strokes

10. Dreams – Fleetwood Mac

I thought "love" meant
keeping their feelings in mind first,
holding in your voice if it meant
it would hurt them too, and accepting
apologies you never received
because you knew they "loved"
you too.

I've since learned it isn't "mean"
to enforce the boundaries
you've made for yourself.
It's okay to walk away
because it isn't love
if they aren't willing to respect them.

When I knew it was ending,
I ripped out the poem "Love Letter"
from my favorite Sylvia Plath collection
and slid it under your pillow.
At the time I didn't have the words
to describe everything that you meant to me.
I just knew I didn't want it to end.

We had a habit of kissing with poems
and making love in between the stanzas.
I was sure the moment you read it
you would remember too.

That day ended up being the last time
we saw each other. I hope
you still have that poem
and that you think of me fondly
every now and again.

We love each other best
when we aren't together.

I'm still learning
the difference
between being
                alone

                                and

                                        loneliness.

The blue lagoon ripples and cries.
I want to love me for a long time.

We only know
a version
of each other
that no longer exists.

I no longer look
for your car on my street
or expect you to show up
at my work with an armful
of apologies and all the things
I've been wanting to hear.

I've learned to accept
the only run-ins with you
will be in my dreams,
and even in those moments
we aren't back together. But,
it sure is a nice surprise
to see your warm smile
and to share the glances
that once made me feel
connected.

I've outgrown you
and sprouted roots
on my own land.
They've soaked
and taken spread
in the dirty soil.
They finally
have the room
to breathe and rise.

Nothing can end me – not even you.

I once brought you back into my life
to help me escape myself.

Little did I know that you leaving
would have me feeling more me
than I've felt in a long time.

I wish I had accepted earlier
that the closure was the pain.

That there would be no apologies,
accountability, or promises
of being better next time.

There would be no reasonable
explanation for how you treated me,
nothing to say to make any of it okay.

That sinking
feeling
in
my gut

was all I should have needed.

I don't want to be resilient,
strong, or any other descriptor
that implies things happen *to* me,
that I must go through, time
and time again.

I want simplicity,
　　　　ease,

a moment
to
just
be.

I'd like to hug the moon now
and cry to the stars.

I do wish you were here,
somewhere in my life.

Sometimes I forget to take care of myself.
I'll lock myself in my room for days,
hyper-focused on perfection. I can feel
my sanity slipping to the edges.
If I can just push through,
next week will be better.
It has to be.

But it isn't.

You've got to feed the body.
You've got to nourish the body.
Give it sunlight.
Bathe it.
Protect it.
Rest it.
Respect it.
That's how it gets better.

How to heal from heartbreak like a poet:

1. Write when you miss them
2. Write when you feel numb
3. Write until it hurts a little less

*Repeat steps as necessary

This Feels Like Home

Long cat stretches,
back bent like a crescent moon,
hands tangled in the grass,
rays hot and golden that blush my skin.

Breathe.

Not everyone is going to leave you.
Not everyone is going to stay.
Neither is a reflection of your worth.

Breathe.

You will be okay.

You are powerful
and strong for making it
to this season of your life.

One day, this
will be the moment
you romanticize
with nostalgia.

Feet grounded in the forest
with the heat of the sun beating.

I can be still. I can just be.
This moment is worth living.

It's so human – that someone you love could also bring you this much pain.

It isn't wrong to set boundaries.
It is a commitment to yourself
        (and to them)
        of healing in love.

                If they deny you and continuously
                break the boundaries you've built,
                        then they are committed
                to control.

Mushrooms

Cosmic fragments
in the teapot.

They blacken and burn
inside the shallow pool.

We take a cup full
to our lips, praying

to the moon
and to the stars. Praying

for gratitude,
acceptance, presence

and a love for this life.
We fall back into the clouds,

levitating. I try to count
each strum and fragment

till the rondo slows, yet
she goes on
turning
and turning.

Let's make out
behind a lava lamp.

Your eyes remind me
of kaleidoscopes

and I'd like to see the teal ooze
levitate hot pink.

Hot Summer

Green lightning bugs,
swamp humid forest,
and the blinking light on beat
fades in and out of my memory.

Across the way you stand
from my window view.
You're so far gone,
yet I can't leave it alone.

That itch
crawls up my legs
and takes me
on a moonlight ride.

I fell into a vortex
in Sedona.

I let the energy carry me away
into another dimension,

one of tranquility and pause.
Here I feel freedom rise in my bones

and cover me with a dry warmth.
Comforting, yet terrifying.

This moment will pass
sure enough.

Disco Dolls

Lime gogo boots
Super moons
Pretty fools
Groovy spirits
Boogie down to fate

Happy Roo

Sticky skin
Glitter eyeshadow
Purple lips
Ocean swirled hair
Hands stuck to the moon sky
Ears mad deaf
I'm high –
Too high for you

*Happy Roo is a greeting at the Bonnaroo music festival. It symbolizes peace, love, and unity.

Cleanse me
under the strawberry moon
until I crystalize.

The moon, on-mouthed
on her back grips tightly
onto the city lights of
Los Angeles. Their beams
gleaning and intertwining.
Ultimately indistinguishable.

Outside myself,
it's pretty to watch.
I think it might be nice
to disappear somewhere deep
into the universe.

Light Up

My ideas are fluid.
Inhale the clouds
in outer space.
Go on, share it
with this strange society
and grin at the lightning
for the next million years.
Sorta hug the feeling
and let her evaporate away
to Jesus.

Zombie Dust

What a strange part of town
we've got here. The black shadows
and the yellow-green moon stars.
I can't explain the vibrations of this place.

I can't slow down now,
there's too far to go.
My head smacks the table and I follow
the pretty stars to Mars
or someplace where you can't follow.
I can see this world is not for you.
So let me run into the galaxy
on my own.

We lay on the red couch outside
in the middle of Joshua Tree.

We take a bag full of magic
and gravitate into the cosmos.

The clouds pop and shake as we travel.
The brass mountains surely follow.
The baby trees groove to a slow burn.

On opposite sides of the couch, we sit
until the oranges of the sky simmer
and fade to a cool black.
The golden stars above –
they blink and bleed glitter.
They hover over me
and let me know it'll be alright.

Here I feel everything
and nothing.

sunset lovers
quiet streets
high tides
salty tongues
lonely nights

everything is temporary.

Grab my crystals
and let me place them
delicately
one by one
on your body.

Lapis lazuli for your forehead.
Agate for your neck.
Opalite for your cheek.
Rose quartz for your chest.

Please. Let me heal the parts
of you that I've hurt.

Hikes through Runyon Canyon,
not quite lush, but high
amongst the mountains
I can dance freely.

The moon will find you.
She'll let you access

    her wisdom and love
    that glow

        from that crescent smile
        even in the darkest of nights.

Golden halos
tremble against
the water. Through
the shine, I examine closer
and see through me into the depths of the sea.

The ocean is one thing that makes me feel safe.
You can trust it'll always
come back to you.

Take me to Joshua Tree
to levitate amongst the mountains.

You'll taste the fire of my skin.
The red dirt, cold and dusty

to the touch
like stardust.

We'll hold this gaze
for eternity.

Alexis Beale is a poet born and raised in Silver Spring, MD (Yes, the same city Stevie Nicks named her song "Silver Springs" after).

Alexis has been writing since age 12 and published her first poem at 17. Her work has appeared in various literary magazines including *Off the Coast, Art + Type, Door is a Jar*, amongst others.

She is a Sagittarius sun and moon, with an Aquarius rising. In her free time, you can find her at concerts or traveling the road.

Connect with her on TikTok or Instagram @alexisbeale_poet